desiderata
Things Desire

Other Books
By Tim Northburg

Decide On It!

Fuel The Furnace

Fuel The Furnace
Workbook

IF – Guiding Principles

Otterocity!

Otterocity!
Field Guide

Realize It!

Realize It!
Goals Workbook

desiderata
Things Desire

A Pocket Guide to Help You
Navigate The Tenants of A Perfect Life

Tim Northburg

desiderata Things Desire

Contents

desiderata Things Desire

Dedication

I dedicate this book to my mom who introduced me to Desiderata. She has a copy of Max Ehrmann's poem hung in her home for many years now. Every time I visit, I read it and it reminds me of what I need to do to live the perfect life. Thanks, Mom.

Preface

In the vast landscape of literature, certain works emerge as timeless treasures, captivating readers across generations with their wisdom and insight. One such masterpiece is the renowned poem "Desiderata" by Max Ehrmann. With its profound words of guidance and solace, this poetic composition has resonated deeply with countless individuals since its creation. In this book, we embark on a journey to unravel the layers of meaning within "Desiderata," and the poems enduring emphasis it has had over the last century.

Max Ehrmann, a native of Terre Haute, Indiana, began crafting this extraordinary work in 1921. However, it was not until 1927 that he bestowed upon it a title by registering it for his U.S. copyright using the poem's opening phrase. The full text of "Desiderata" was finally published on the cover of the April 5, 1933 issue of Michigan Tradesman magazine, with Ehrmann acknowledged as its author. It was during this time that the poem gained its rightful recognition and began its remarkable journey through the annals of literary history.

The true significance of "Desiderata" became apparent during the tumultuous years of World War II. Psychiatrist Merrill Moore, recognizing the poem's therapeutic value, distributed over a thousand copies to his patients and soldiers, offering them solace and strength amidst the chaos of war. Sadly, Max Ehrmann passed away in 1945, leaving behind a profound legacy with "Desiderata" as one of his most celebrated creations. It was his widow who, in 1948, published the poem as part of The Poems of Max Ehrmann. This publication solidified the poem's place in the hearts of readers worldwide.

As fate would have it, "Desiderata" encountered another turning point in its journey when Reverend Frederick Kates shared it with his congregation at Old Saint Paul's Church in Baltimore around 1959 or 1960. Approximately 200 copies of the poem were distributed anonymously, adding a touch of mystery to its origins. Unfortunately, the mention of the church's foundation date of 1692 on these papers led to a false assumption regarding the poem's origination. Nonetheless, this inadvertent association only served to deepen the enigmatic allure surrounding "Desiderata."

desiderata Things Desire

In this book, we delve into the intricate tapestry of "Desiderata," examining its timeless themes, universal wisdom, and profound insights. We explore the ways in which its messages of inner peace, resilience, and authenticity have transcended time and resonated with countless souls. Through a meticulous analysis of the poem's words, we hope to unveil the hidden gems of wisdom that lie within, empowering readers to embrace its teachings and apply them to their own lives.

Join us as we embark on this enlightening exploration of "Desiderata" and discover why, even after a century, its enduring relevance continues to captivate and inspire us all.

Desiderata

Go placidly amid the noise and the haste, and remember what peace there may be in silence. As far as possible, without surrender, be on good terms with all persons.

Speak your truth quietly and clearly; and listen to others, even to the dull and the ignorant; they too have their story.

Avoid loud and aggressive persons; they are vexatious to the spirit. If you compare yourself with others, you may become vain or bitter, for always there will be greater and lesser persons than yourself.

Enjoy your achievements as well as your plans. Keep interested in your own career, however humble; it is a real possession in the changing fortunes of time.

Exercise caution in your business affairs, for the world is full of trickery. But let this not blind you to what virtue there is; many persons strive for high ideals, and everywhere life is full of heroism.

Be yourself. Especially do not feign affection. Neither be cynical about love; for in the face of all aridity and disenchantment, it is as perennial as the grass.

Take kindly the counsel of the years, gracefully surrendering the things of youth.

Nurture strength of spirit to shield you in sudden misfortune. But do not distress yourself with dark imaginings. Many fears are born of fatigue and loneliness.

Beyond a wholesome discipline, be gentle with yourself. You are a child of the universe no less than the trees and the stars; you have a right to be here.

And whether or not it is clear to you, no doubt the universe is unfolding as it should.

Therefore be at peace with God, whatever you conceive Him to be. And whatever your labors and aspirations, in the noisy confusion of life, keep peace in your soul.

With all its sham, drudgery and broken dreams, it is still a beautiful world. Be cheerful. Strive to be happy.

By Max Ehrmann 1927

desiderata Things Desire

Unveiling Desiderata

In a world that is constantly evolving, where the pace of life seems to quicken with each passing day, it is crucial for us to pause and reflect upon the timeless wisdom that can guide us towards a fulfilling and successful life. Among the myriad of insights and teachings that have stood the test of time, there is a profound poem that resonates deeply with the human spirit — "Desiderata."

Desiderata, Latin for "things desired." It is also interpreted as "things wanted" or "things needed." Desiderata is a poetic masterpiece that encapsulates a powerful message: to approach life with a positive outlook and to recognize the inherent worth and purpose within ourselves and every individual we encounter. Written by Max Ehrmann in the early 1920s, this timeless piece of literature continues to inspire and motivate individuals across generations, serving as a beacon of hope in a world often filled with chaos and uncertainty.

desiderata Things Desire

At its core, the poem "Desiderata" reminds us that we are all children of the universe, belonging to a grand tapestry woven by a higher power. Each and every one of us has a unique purpose, an irreplaceable role to play in the symphony of life. In an era where individualism and self-expression are celebrated, it is crucial to remember that our lives are intricately connected to those around us. We must strive to maintain harmony and goodwill in our interactions, cultivating relationships built on empathy, understanding, and respect.

Living in today's society, it is easy to be consumed by the noise and distractions that bombard us from every direction. We find ourselves caught up in the pursuit of material success, often neglecting the essence of what it truly means to live a perfect life. However, the essence of Desiderata is as relevant today as it was when it was first penned down over a hundred years ago. Its message serves as a gentle reminder to slow down, to appreciate the simple pleasures that surround us, and to find joy in the present moment.

Moreover, Desiderata compels us to listen and to not merely to hear the words that are spoken, but to truly understand and empathize with the experiences and perspectives of others. In a society where communication has been reduced to sound bites and social media posts, the art of deep listening is often overlooked. Yet, by honoring the stories of those around us, even if they may seem mundane, we foster a sense of interconnectedness and forge meaningful connections that enrich our own lives.

As we navigate the complexities of the modern world, it is easy to succumb to despair and cynicism. Yet, Desiderata reminds us that despite the challenges we face, the world remains a beautiful place. It is a call to action, inviting us to embrace life with honesty and cheerfulness, and to appreciate the wonders that unfold before us. By nurturing a positive mindset and embracing the inherent goodness of humanity, we can create a ripple effect that touches the lives of others and contributes to a more harmonious and fulfilling society.

In the pages that follow, we will explore the profound wisdom of Desiderata and uncover its relevance in today's fast-paced and demanding world. We will delve into the principles and practices that can help us lead lives filled with purpose, authenticity, and joy. Through real-life examples and practical strategies, we will embark on a transformative journey, unlocking the secrets to living a perfect life, as envisioned by Desiderata.

So, let us embark on this extraordinary voyage, embracing the wisdom of the ages and charting a course towards a life that is abundant, meaningful, and true. Together, let us discover the path to success and fulfillment as we navigate the complexities of the modern world, guided by the timeless teachings of Desiderata.

*"Go placidly amid the noise
and the haste,"*

Perfect Life Amid Chaos

In today's fast-paced and ever-evolving society, the phrase "Go placidly amid the noise and haste" holds more significance than ever before. Our lives are filled with incessant distractions, constant demands, and an overwhelming sense of urgency. It is all too easy to get caught up in the chaos, losing sight of what truly matters and losing ourselves in the process. This chapter aims to explore the relevance of this timeless wisdom in our modern world and uncover the secrets to living a perfect life amidst the chaos.

In a society driven by instant gratification and superficial achievements, it is crucial to take a step back and reflect on the true essence of a perfect life. It is not about accumulating material possessions or chasing after fleeting pleasures. Instead, it is about finding peace, fulfillment, and authenticity within ourselves.

To "go placidly" means to cultivate a sense of inner calm and tranquility, even in the midst of external chaos. It involves embracing mindfulness and practicing self-care to nourish our mental, emotional, and physical well-being. In a world where noise bombards us from every direction, it is essential to create moments of silence and solitude, allowing us to reconnect with our inner selves. Taking time for introspection, meditation, or simply enjoying the beauty of nature can help us regain clarity and perspective.

Similarly, to navigate the 'haste' that permeates our society, we must learn the art of deliberate living. It is easy to fall into the trap of busyness, constantly rushing from one task to another without purpose or intention. However, a perfect life is not defined by how much we accomplish or how many items we tick off our to-do list. It is about focusing on what truly matters, aligning our actions with our values, and prioritizing our well-being and relationships above all else.

In the face of societal pressures and external expectations, it takes courage to march to the beat of our own drum. To live a perfect life, we must be willing to question the status quo and redefine success on our own terms. It means embracing our unique talents, passions, and values, and aligning our actions with our authentic selves. It is about creating a life that resonates with our deepest desires, rather than conforming to societal norms.

Living a perfect life also involves nurturing meaningful connections with others. Despite the prevalence of virtual interactions and superficial connections, true happiness lies in cultivating genuine relationships and fostering a sense of belonging. Taking the time to connect with loved ones, being present in their lives, and showing empathy and kindness can enrich our own lives in immeasurable ways.

The timeless wisdom of "Go placidly amid the noise and haste" is more relevant today than ever before. It serves as a reminder to find solace within ourselves amidst the chaos of modern life. By embracing mindfulness, deliberate living, authenticity, and meaningful connections, we can create a life that is truly perfect for us. It is a journey that requires self-reflection, courage, and a commitment to our own well-being and happiness. So, let us embark on this path, and may we find serenity and fulfillment in the midst of the noise and haste.

"and remember what peace there may be in silence."

Silent Power Within Us

Silence is a rare and often undervalued commodity. Our lives are filled with constant noise—the ringing of phones, the pinging of notifications, the hum of traffic, and the clamor of busy minds. We have become accustomed to a relentless assault on our senses, leaving little room for peace and tranquility.

Yet, amidst the chaos, there is profound wisdom in the age-old adage: "Remember what peace there may be in silence." In a world that constantly demands our attention, finding moments of stillness becomes an essential practice for our overall well-being and success. Let us explore what this means in the context of our modern society and how we can harness the power of silence to create a life that feels truly perfect.

Silence is not just the absence of sound; it is a sanctuary for reflection, self-discovery, and personal growth. In the midst of our busy lives, we must intentionally seek out silence and give ourselves permission to pause, detach from the external distractions, and connect with our inner selves. It is within the silence that we can gain clarity, find solace, and tap into our deepest reservoirs of creativity and intuition.

Today, where technology has made constant connectivity the norm, finding silence can seem like a daunting task. However, it is precisely in this digital age that we must be more intentional about cultivating moments of quietude. We can start by creating sacred spaces in our daily routines where we intentionally unplug from the world and give ourselves the gift of silence. It could be as simple as sitting alone in nature, meditating, journaling, or engaging in activities that bring us peace and solitude.

When we embrace silence, we create a fertile ground for self-reflection and self-awareness. In the quiet moments, we can take stock of our lives, examine our values, and reflect on our goals and aspirations. It is within these introspective moments that we gain insight into what truly matters to us and align our actions with our deepest desires. Silence allows us to listen to the whispers of our souls, helping us make decisions that resonate with our authentic selves.

Moreover, silence opens the doors to deeper connections with others. In a society that often values loudness and constant stimulation, truly listening becomes a rare gift. When we engage in mindful silence, we become present for others, offering them our undivided attention and creating a space for them to be heard and understood. By practicing active listening and honoring the power of silence in our conversations, we foster deeper connections, empathy, and mutual respect.

In our pursuit of a perfect life, we must remember that perfection is not found in external achievements alone. It is in the moments of silence that we discover our inner strengths, our passions, and our purpose. By embracing silence, we cultivate the ability to navigate the noise of the world with grace and discernment. We become more resilient, more centered, and more attuned to our own needs and the needs of those around us.

So, let us remember what peace there may be in silence. Let us make space in our lives for stillness, reflection, and connection. In the quietude, we find the wisdom and clarity to lead lives that are not only successful but also deeply fulfilling. As we embrace silence as a guiding principle, we unlock the true potential within ourselves and create a path towards living a perfect life—a life that is authentic, purposeful, and in harmony with our true selves.

"As far as possible, without surrender, be on good terms with all persons."

Living In Harmony

Navigating relationships and maintaining a harmonious environment can be quite challenging. Nevertheless, the principle of being on good terms with all persons remains as relevant as ever. It is a testament to the power of compassion, empathy, and understanding in fostering personal growth, success, and overall well-being.

In a world where diverse perspectives and ideologies coexist, conflicts and disagreements are inevitable. However, the key lies in how we approach and manage these differences. Being on good terms with all persons does not imply sacrificing our own values or compromising our authenticity. It is about embracing the art of effective communication, conflict resolution, and building bridges rather than walls.

To embody this principle in today's society, it is crucial to develop certain qualities and adopt specific strategies that promote positive interactions. Here are some key insights to help you navigate the intricacies of modern relationships and foster a life of fulfillment:

Cultivate Empathy and Open-mindedness: Empathy is the cornerstone of understanding and connecting with others. By putting yourself in someone else's shoes, you gain valuable insights into their perspectives, experiences, and emotions. Approach conversations and interactions with an open mind, free from judgment and preconceived notions. This attitude encourages mutual respect and allows for constructive dialogue.

Communicate with Clarity and Respect: Effective communication is the bedrock of any healthy relationship. Be mindful of your words, tone, and body language when expressing your thoughts or addressing conflicts. Articulate your ideas with clarity, focusing on the issue at hand rather than attacking the individual. Active listening is equally important—give others the opportunity to express themselves fully, showing genuine interest and respect for their viewpoints.

Seek Common Ground: While we all possess unique backgrounds and beliefs, there is often common ground to be found. Instead of fixating on differences, actively seek areas of agreement or shared goals. Identifying common interests promotes unity and collaboration, paving the way for constructive relationships even in the face of diverse opinions.

Practice Forgiveness and Letting Go: Holding grudges and harboring negativity only hinders personal growth and disrupts relationships. Learn to forgive and let go of past grievances, freeing yourself from the burdens of resentment. Remember, forgiveness does not mean forgetting or condoning the actions of others—it is a step towards your own peace and emotional well-being.

Embrace Diversity and Inclusivity: Our society thrives on diversity, and embracing it enriches our lives in countless ways. Celebrate the uniqueness of individuals around you, regardless of their cultural, social, or ideological backgrounds. Foster an inclusive environment that values different perspectives, as it leads to innovation, creativity, and personal growth.

Set Healthy Boundaries: While it is crucial to strive for positive relationships, it is equally important to establish healthy boundaries. Boundaries help protect your mental and emotional well-being, ensuring that you maintain a healthy sense of self while engaging with others. Learn to recognize when a relationship becomes toxic or detrimental to your growth and be willing to step back when necessary.

desiderata Things Desire

Practice Self-reflection and Personal Growth: Building and maintaining healthy relationships requires continuous self-reflection and personal growth. Regularly assess your own attitudes, biases, and behaviors, striving to improve and evolve. Recognize that nobody is perfect, and personal growth is a lifelong journey. By continually working on yourself, you become better equipped to navigate relationships and positively impact the lives of those around you.

Being on good terms with all persons means embracing the complexities of human relationships and striving for understanding, compassion, and respect. By embodying these principles, you not only enhance your own personal growth but also contribute to a more harmonious and inclusive world. Remember, the pursuit of a perfect life lies not in the absence of conflicts but in the ability to navigate them with grace and integrity.

"Speak your truth quietly and clearly; and listen to others, even to the dull and the ignorant; they too have their story."

Balance In Communication

In today's fast-paced and interconnected society, the importance of speaking your truth quietly and clearly has never been more relevant. We live in a world where information travels at lightning speed, where opinions are voiced with fervor, and where it's easy to get caught up in the noise of it all. But amidst this chaos, it is crucial to find your voice, express your thoughts authentically, and listen to others with empathy and understanding.

Speaking your truth quietly and clearly means having the courage to express your beliefs, ideas, and values, even in the face of opposition or indifference. It is about standing up for what you believe in, not with the intention of overpowering others, but with the aim of contributing to a meaningful conversation. Your words carry weight, and by articulating your truth calmly and respectfully, you create a space for genuine dialogue and understanding.

However, speaking your truth quietly and clearly should not be mistaken for silence or passivity. It is not about suppressing your voice or holding back your opinions. Instead, it is an invitation to engage in thoughtful and constructive communication, acknowledging that the volume of your voice does not determine the validity of your perspective. In a society where shouting and divisiveness often dominate, the power of a quiet and clear voice can be transformative.

In the process of speaking your truth, it is equally important to listen to others, even those you may consider dull or ignorant. Our society is diverse, composed of individuals from various backgrounds, experiences, and knowledge levels. Each person has a unique story to tell, and by lending an ear, you open yourself up to a world of insights and perspectives that can broaden your own understanding.

Listening to others, regardless of their intelligence or knowledge, requires empathy and an open mind. It means seeking to understand before being understood, setting aside preconceived notions, and genuinely considering alternative viewpoints. Every person has their own context and life experiences, which shape their beliefs and perspectives. By taking the time to listen and appreciate these stories, we cultivate empathy, bridge divides, and foster a sense of unity in our society.

In a world increasingly driven by polarization and echo chambers, it is vital to break free from these self-imposed constraints. Engaging in meaningful conversations with those who have different opinions or seem less informed opens up opportunities for personal growth and societal progress. By valuing diverse perspectives, we create an environment where knowledge, ideas, and wisdom can flow freely, leading to innovative solutions and a more harmonious society.

Living a perfect life is not about being surrounded only by like-minded individuals or ignoring those we consider less knowledgeable. It is about embracing the richness of human experience, valuing every individual's story, and finding common ground amidst our differences. Speaking your truth quietly and clearly, while listening to others, allows you to contribute meaningfully to the world, foster understanding, and shape a society that values dialogue, empathy, and personal growth.

As you navigate the complexities of our modern society, remember that your voice matters. Embrace the power of speaking your truth with humility and respect. Likewise, be open to listening and learning from others, regardless of their background or level of knowledge. In doing so, you will not only enrich your own life but also contribute to a society that cherishes authenticity, empathy, and the diverse tapestry of human stories.

"Avoid loud and aggressive persons; they are vexatious to the spirit."

Avoid Toxic Influences

In our journey towards living a perfect life, it is essential to surround ourselves with positive influences and avoid those who drain our energy. The timeless wisdom encapsulated in the verse "Avoid loud and aggressive persons; they are vexatious to the spirit" holds even more significance in today's society, where negativity and aggression seem to pervade various aspects of our lives.

In a world saturated with constant noise and opinions, it is crucial to filter out the negative influences that can hinder our growth and diminish our spirits. Loudness, in this context, goes beyond just the volume of someone's voice. It refers to individuals who project their negativity, aggression, and pessimism onto others, seeking to bring them down rather than lifting them up.

Unfortunately, our society is no stranger to loud and aggressive personalities. They might be found in the workplace, social circles, or even within our families. Their behavior can take many forms: they might constantly criticize, belittle, or verbally attack others. They thrive on conflict and drama, leaving a trail of negativity in their wake. Engaging with such individuals not only drains our energy but also hampers our ability to focus on personal growth and success.

To live a perfect life, it is essential to create an environment that nourishes our spirit and fuels our aspirations. Here are some strategies to navigate the presence of loud and aggressive individuals in today's society:

Practice Emotional Intelligence: It is crucial to develop emotional intelligence and learn to recognize and manage our own emotions when confronted with loud and aggressive personalities. By maintaining self-awareness and controlling our reactions, we can prevent their negative energy from affecting us.

Set Boundaries: Establishing clear boundaries is key to protecting our well-being. Learn to say no to toxic interactions and limit your exposure to individuals who consistently exhibit loud and aggressive behavior. Remember, it is within your power to choose who you surround yourself with.

Seek Positive Relationships: Surround yourself with individuals who inspire, uplift, and support you. Seek out positive relationships that foster personal growth, motivate you to reach your goals, and celebrate your achievements. These individuals will nourish your spirit and help you thrive.

Cultivate Inner Strength: Building resilience and cultivating inner strength is essential to combat the negative impact of loud and aggressive individuals. Focus on your personal development, engage in activities that bring you joy, and prioritize self-care. By strengthening your inner self, you become less vulnerable to external negativity.

Lead by Example: Instead of being consumed by the negativity around you, strive to be a positive influence on others. Lead by example, practicing kindness, empathy, and respect. Your actions can inspire those around you to follow suit, creating a ripple effect of positivity in our society.

Today, the admonition to avoid loud and aggressive persons holds even greater significance. By consciously choosing to distance ourselves from negativity, we create the space necessary for personal growth, happiness, and success. Remember, it is up to us to shape our environments and nourish our spirits with positivity, compassion, and empathy.

"If you compare yourself with others, you may become vain or bitter, for always there will be greater and lesser persons than yourself."

desiderata **Things Desire**

Self-Imposter Syndrome

The phenomenon of comparison has become more prevalent than ever before. We find ourselves constantly bombarded with carefully curated images and stories of people's successes, achievements, and seemingly perfect lives through various social media platforms. It has become all too easy to fall into the trap of comparing our own lives to those we see online, often leading to feelings of inadequacy, jealousy, and a distorted sense of self-worth. However, the wisdom behind the title of this chapter remains as relevant today as it ever was.

To live a perfect life, it is crucial to understand that comparison can be a double-edged sword. On one hand, it can serve as a powerful source of inspiration and motivation. Seeing others achieve great things can ignite a fire within us, pushing us to strive for our own goals and reach new heights. Witnessing someone else's success can act as a reminder that greatness is possible and that we too are capable of accomplishing remarkable things.

On the other hand, constant comparison can lead to negative consequences. When we compare ourselves to others and find ourselves falling short, it can breed feelings of vanity or bitterness. Vanity arises when we believe ourselves to be superior to others, basing our self-worth solely on our perceived successes in comparison to theirs. This path leads to an inflated ego that ultimately isolates us from genuine connections and personal growth.

Conversely, bitterness takes hold when we constantly find ourselves lacking in comparison to others. We become consumed by envy, resentment, and self-doubt, which hinder our ability to appreciate our own accomplishments and find joy in our unique journey. Bitterness robs us of the opportunity to celebrate the progress we have made and blinds us to the abundant blessings in our own lives.

To break free from the detrimental cycle of comparison, we must shift our focus inward and embrace a mindset of self-acceptance and gratitude. Recognize that every individual's path is different, and comparison serves no purpose other than to distract us from our own potential. Embrace the truth that success is subjective and personal, defined by our own values and aspirations.

desiderata Things Desire

Instead of comparing ourselves to others, let us strive for self-improvement and growth. Set goals that align with our passions and values and measure our progress against our own benchmarks. Celebrate every milestone, no matter how small, and appreciate the unique talents and strengths that make us who we are.

Moreover, let us learn from the achievements of others without falling into the trap of comparison. Surround ourselves with individuals who inspire us and offer guidance and support. Instead of feeling threatened by their success, use it as an opportunity to learn from their experiences and seek guidance on our own journey.

Living a perfect life does not mean reaching a state of flawlessness or achieving constant external validation. It is about embracing our own individuality, pursuing our passions, and finding fulfillment in our own unique journey. By letting go of the need to compare ourselves to others, we can cultivate a deep sense of self-worth, contentment, and joy.

Remember, life is not a competition against others; it is a journey of self-discovery and personal growth. Embrace your own path, celebrate your achievements, and appreciate the journey as it unfolds. The only person you should compare yourself to is the person you were yesterday. Strive to become the best

version of yourself and let that be your measure
of success.

"Enjoy your achievements as well as your plans."

Enjoy The Journey

In our fast-paced society, where hustle and constant striving for success have become the norm, it's easy to get caught up in a perpetual cycle of chasing after goals and ambitions. We often find ourselves relentlessly pursuing the next milestone, believing that true fulfillment lies solely in reaching the pinnacle of our aspirations. However, in our relentless pursuit, we may forget a fundamental truth: Life is not only about the destination; it's about the journey and appreciating every step along the way.

The pressure to achieve and the fear of missing out have never been more prevalent. We're bombarded with images of glamorous lifestyles and seemingly perfect lives on social media, leading us to compare our own progress with others constantly. The danger in this mindset is that we become so fixated on future accomplishments that we overlook the significance of our present achievements and the progress we have already made.

desiderata Things Desire

Enjoying your achievements as well as your plans means finding joy and contentment in the present moment while still working towards your goals. It's about acknowledging and celebrating how far you've come, the obstacles you've overcome, and the lessons you've learned along the way. It's recognizing that every step, whether big or small, is a testament to your growth and personal development.

Living a perfect life does not mean a life devoid of challenges or failures. It's an understanding that perfection is subjective and that true fulfillment comes from embracing imperfections and appreciating the beauty in life's unpredictability. It's about finding balance and being kind to yourself in the pursuit of your dreams.

So, how can we apply this principle in today's society?

First and foremost, cultivate gratitude for the journey you're on. Take a moment each day to reflect on your accomplishments, both big and small. Whether it's landing a new job, completing a project, or even making progress in your personal life, acknowledge and celebrate these achievements. Recognize the effort, dedication, and resilience it took to get there.

Secondly, practice mindfulness and be fully present in the moment. Often, our minds are preoccupied with future plans, worries, and aspirations. By grounding ourselves in the present, we can fully experience and savor the joys and pleasures that surround us. Find moments of stillness amidst the chaos, whether it's through meditation, spending time in nature, or engaging in activities that bring you peace and fulfillment.

Additionally, remember that success is not a linear path. It's essential to set goals and have a vision for your future, but allow yourself to be flexible and open to new possibilities. Embrace detours and unexpected opportunities that may arise along your journey. Sometimes, unplanned experiences can lead to the most profound personal growth and fulfillment.

Lastly, surround yourself with a supportive community. Share your achievements with loved ones who genuinely celebrate your successes and lift you up during challenging times. Connect with like-minded individuals who understand the value of enjoying the present and encourage you to celebrate your accomplishments. Building a network of positive influences can greatly enhance your overall well-being and perspective on success.

Enjoying your achievements as well as your plans is a vital component of living a perfect life in today's society. By practicing gratitude, mindfulness, flexibility, and surrounding yourself with a supportive community, you can find fulfillment in the journey and appreciate the progress you've made. Remember, life is not a race to the finish line; it's a collection of meaningful moments and personal growth. So, celebrate your achievements, embrace the present, and continue to strive for your dreams while savoring the beauty of the present moment.

*"Keep interested in your own
career, however humble; it is
a real possession in the
changing fortunes of time."*

Maintain Career Passion

The notion of a "perfect life" can be elusive and even misleading. The definition of success varies from person to person, and societal expectations often overshadow individual aspirations. However, amidst the chaos and noise, one timeless principle remains true: the importance of staying interested and invested in your own career, regardless of its perceived status or humble beginnings.

Rapid technological advancements and economic shifts constantly reshape industries and job markets. The significance of maintaining a genuine interest in your chosen career path cannot be overstated. Embracing this mindset empowers you to navigate the changing fortunes of time with resilience, adaptability, and a sense of purpose. Here's what it means to keep interested in your own career today:

Seek Growth and Learning Opportunities: Regardless of your field or position, there is always room for growth and improvement. Embrace a growth mindset that fuels your curiosity and pushes you to continually expand your knowledge and skill set. In today's dynamic landscape, industries are constantly evolving, and staying up to date with emerging trends and technologies is crucial. Attend workshops, enroll in courses, join professional networks, and seek mentorship to enhance your expertise. Remember, the pursuit of knowledge is a lifelong journey that enriches both your personal and professional growth.

Embrace Change and Adaptability: The changing fortunes of time often bring unforeseen challenges and opportunities. The ability to adapt and embrace change is vital for long-term success. In a rapidly evolving society, industries that once seemed invincible can become obsolete, and new ones can emerge seemingly overnight. By staying interested in your own career, you remain attuned to these shifts and proactively prepare yourself for the changing landscape. Be open to exploring new roles, industries, and even entrepreneurial endeavors if they align with your passions and values. Embracing change allows you to stay relevant and seize opportunities that come your way.

Cultivate a Sense of Purpose: Beyond monetary rewards and societal recognition, finding meaning and purpose in your career is a key ingredient for a fulfilling life. When you are genuinely interested in your work, you are more likely to experience a sense of purpose and satisfaction. Reflect on your values, passions, and the positive impact you want to make through your career. Identify how your unique skills and talents can contribute to a greater cause or help others. When you align your career with your values, you create a deeper connection to your work and find meaning even in the humblest of roles.

Foster Resilience and Perseverance: Living a perfect life does not imply a smooth and effortless journey. Challenges, setbacks, and failures are an inevitable part of any career path. However, maintaining a genuine interest in your work provides you with the resilience and perseverance needed to overcome obstacles. When you are passionate about what you do, setbacks become learning opportunities, failures become steppingstones, and adversities become catalysts for growth. Embrace a mindset of resilience and view each challenge as an opportunity to develop new skills, gain valuable experience, and strengthen your character.

Cultivate Work-Life Balance: In the pursuit of professional success, it is essential to maintain a healthy work-life balance. While it is crucial to stay interested and invested in your career, it should not come at the expense of your well-being, relationships, and personal growth. Prioritize self-care, maintain strong personal connections, and engage in activities that bring you joy and fulfillment outside of work. Remember that a harmonious balance between your career and personal life enhances overall satisfaction and contributes to your long-term success.

The idea of a perfect life may be subjective and elusive. However, keeping interested in your own career, however humble, remains a timeless principle. By seeking growth, embracing change, cultivating a sense of purpose, fostering resilience, and maintaining a healthy work-life balance, you can navigate the changing fortunes of time with grace and success. Remember, your career is a real possession that can bring you fulfillment, personal growth, and contribute to the betterment of society. Stay interested, stay motivated, and live a life aligned with your passions and values.

"Exercise caution in your business affairs, for the world is full of trickery."

Caution In Business Affairs

Where innovation, entrepreneurship, and business opportunities are abound, it is more crucial than ever to exercise caution in your business affairs. The verse "for the world is full of trickery" has taken on a whole new meaning in our fast-paced, interconnected world. While it is an exciting time to pursue your dreams and create success, it is equally important to be aware of the pitfalls and deceptions that can arise along the way.

Recognizing Deceptive Practices: The first step in exercising caution is to educate yourself about the various deceptive practices that exist in the business world. From fraudulent schemes to unethical practices, there are individuals and organizations who will stop at nothing to achieve their own gains at the expense of others. Being informed about common scams, deceptive marketing tactics, and unethical business practices will enable you to navigate the intricate web of the business world more effectively.

Trust Your Gut Instincts: In the pursuit of success, it is easy to get caught up in the allure of grand promises and quick wins. However, always trust your gut instincts when something feels too good to be true. If a business opportunity or partnership seems too easy or if you sense a lack of transparency, take a step back and thoroughly evaluate the situation. Intuition can often be a powerful guide and can save you from falling into the traps set by those who seek to deceive.

Do Your Due Diligence: Before entering into any business deal or partnership, conduct thorough research and due diligence. Investigate the background and reputation of individuals or companies you are considering working with. Look for reviews, testimonials, and references from trusted sources. Verify credentials, licenses, and certifications. By arming yourself with accurate information, you will be better equipped to make informed decisions and avoid potential pitfalls.

Build a Network of Trustworthy Allies: Surrounding yourself with a network of trustworthy individuals is invaluable in the business world. Seek out mentors, advisors, and colleagues who have a proven track record of integrity and success. Their guidance and insights can help you navigate challenging situations and make wise decisions. Additionally, they can provide referrals to reputable professionals and assist you in detecting potential scams or deceptive practices.

Continuous Learning and Adaptation: In a rapidly evolving business landscape, knowledge and adaptability are paramount. Stay updated with industry trends, emerging technologies, and changing regulations. Attend seminars, workshops, and conferences to expand your knowledge and network. By staying informed and adaptable, you will be better equipped to identify potential risks and adapt your strategies accordingly.

Cultivate Ethical Business Practices: While the world may be full of trickery, it does not mean that you have to succumb to unethical practices. Maintain your integrity and cultivate a reputation for ethical business practices. Honesty, transparency, and fairness should be the cornerstones of your entrepreneurial journey. When you uphold these values, you build trust with customers, partners, and stakeholders, which ultimately leads to long-term success.

Remember, caution does not equate to fear or inaction. Instead, it empowers you to navigate the complex and sometimes treacherous waters of the business world with prudence and wisdom. By exercising caution, trusting your instincts, and staying informed, you can protect yourself and your endeavors from those who seek to deceive. Embrace the challenges, learn from the setbacks, and continue to pursue your dreams with integrity. Success in both business and life lies not only in achieving your goals but also in doing so with a clear conscience and an unwavering commitment to ethical conduct.

"But let this not blind you to what virtue there is; many persons strive for high ideals, and everywhere life is full of heroism."

desiderata Things Desire

Virtue And Heroism

In our fast-paced and often tumultuous society, it's easy to get caught up in the pursuit of a perfect life. We are bombarded with images of success, happiness, and fulfillment at every turn, making it seem as though perfection is the ultimate goal. However, in our quest for perfection, we must not allow ourselves to become blind to the virtues that exist around us and the countless individuals who strive for high ideals. Moreover, we must recognize that heroism is not confined to grand acts of bravery but can be found in the everyday struggles and triumphs of ordinary people.

Today, the concept of virtue may seem outdated or even naive. We are often confronted with stories of corruption, greed, and moral failings, which can lead us to believe that virtue is a rare and unattainable quality. However, it is precisely in the face of these challenges that virtue shines brightest. It is in the small acts of kindness, integrity, and compassion that we can find inspiration and hope.

Many individuals today are striving for high ideals, despite the obstacles they face. They are dedicated to making a positive impact on the world, whether through their work, personal relationships, or involvement in their communities. These individuals understand that success is not solely measured by external accomplishments or material wealth but by the fulfillment that comes from living in alignment with their values.

While heroism may bring to mind images of superheroes and larger-than-life figures, it is crucial to recognize that heroism exists in everyday life. Heroism can be found in the single parent working tirelessly to provide for their children, in the teacher who goes above and beyond to inspire their students, or in the healthcare worker who selflessly cares for the sick and vulnerable. Heroism is present in the quiet determination of individuals who face adversity with resilience and grace.

Our society often places undue emphasis on external achievements and the pursuit of perfection, leading us to overlook the virtues and heroism that exist in our midst. We must shift our focus to recognize and celebrate these qualities, for they are the bedrock of a meaningful and fulfilling life.

To embrace this perspective, we can start by cultivating a sense of gratitude and appreciation for the virtues we witness in others and within ourselves. By acknowledging and valuing acts of kindness, honesty, and selflessness, we can create a ripple effect that encourages others to embody these virtues as well.

Additionally, we should seek out stories of everyday heroes, individuals who have overcome adversity and made a positive impact on their communities. By highlighting these stories and celebrating their achievements, we can inspire others to believe in their own capacity for heroism and strive for their own high ideals.

Living a perfect life does not mean striving for an unattainable ideal, but rather embracing the imperfect and recognizing the beauty that lies within it. It means cherishing the virtues that are present in ourselves and others, and finding inspiration in the everyday heroism that surrounds us.

As we navigate the complexities of modern society, let us not be blinded by the allure of perfection. Instead, let us open our eyes to the virtues that exist, the high ideals that are pursued, and the heroism that permeates every corner of our lives. By doing so, we can create a world that is not only successful and accomplished but also compassionate, resilient, and truly fulfilling.

"Be yourself."

Embrace Your Authenticity

In our fast-paced and ever-evolving society, the pressure to conform and fit into predefined molds has become increasingly prevalent. We are bombarded with images and messages telling us how we should look, what we should do, and who we should be. In the midst of this, it is more crucial than ever to embrace the concept of "Be Yourself." This chapter explores the significance of being authentic and true to yourself in a world that often encourages conformity.

Embracing Authenticity: Being yourself means embracing your true essence, quirks, flaws, and all. It involves recognizing and accepting who you are at your core, rather than striving to be a replica of someone else. Each of us is unique, with our own set of talents, passions, and perspectives. Embracing authenticity means living in alignment with your values, interests, and aspirations, even if they don't align with societal expectations.

Overcoming the Fear of Judgment: One of the biggest barriers to being yourself is the fear of judgment. Society can be quick to criticize and label those who deviate from the norm. However, it's essential to recognize that the opinions of others do not define your worth or dictate your path. The fear of judgment often stems from a desire for acceptance and fitting in. But it's important to remember that true acceptance and fulfillment come from embracing your unique self, rather than trying to please others.

Finding Your Passion and Purpose: Being yourself also involves discovering and pursuing your passion and purpose in life. When you align your actions with your true interests and talents, you experience a sense of fulfillment and joy that cannot be replicated. Take the time to explore different areas, try new things, and reflect on what truly brings you alive. By following your own path, you contribute your unique gifts to the world and create a life of purpose and meaning.

Resisting Comparison: In a society driven by social media, comparison has become an ever-present challenge. It's effortless to fall into the trap of comparing our lives, achievements, and appearances with others, leading to feelings of inadequacy and self-doubt. Being yourself requires resisting this urge to compare and recognizing that your journey is unique. Remember that social media often showcases curated highlights, not the full reality. Focus on your own growth and progress rather than comparing yourself to others.

Embracing Diversity and Inclusion: Being yourself goes beyond just accepting and embracing your own individuality; it also involves celebrating and supporting the uniqueness of others. Our society thrives on diversity, and by embracing different perspectives, backgrounds, and experiences, we foster innovation, creativity, and compassion. Actively promote inclusivity, challenge stereotypes, and cultivate an environment where everyone feels valued and accepted for who they truly are.

In a society that often imposes expectations and pressures, embracing the concept of "Be Yourself" is a powerful act of self-love and personal empowerment. By being authentic, you create a life that is aligned with your values, passions, and purpose. Remember that you are a unique individual, and your journey is yours alone. Embrace your true self, resist the fear of judgment, and celebrate the diversity of those around you. By living authentically, you inspire others to do the same and contribute to a more inclusive and compassionate society.

"Especially do not feign affection."

True Connections

In today's society, where connections are often forged through screens and social media profiles, the notion of feigning affection has become increasingly prevalent. The pressure to maintain a perfect facade, to present a flawless image of ourselves to the world, has created a culture where authenticity often takes a backseat. However, living a perfect life requires more than just a carefully crafted illusion—it demands genuine connections and sincere emotions.

Authenticity is the cornerstone of a fulfilling existence. It means being true to yourself and expressing your thoughts, feelings, and beliefs without pretense or artifice. It is about embracing your flaws, acknowledging your vulnerabilities, and allowing others to see the real you. When you feign affection, you deny yourself the opportunity for genuine connections and rob others of the chance to truly know you.

In the age of social media, it has become all too easy to construct a facade, to curate an idealized version of ourselves for public consumption. We meticulously edit our photos, carefully choose the moments we share, and filter our lives to present an airbrushed reality. But behind the filters and perfectly posed smiles, a hollow emptiness can grow. The more we hide behind these illusions, the further we drift from genuine human connection.

Living a perfect life is not about projecting an image of flawlessness but about embracing imperfections as an integral part of our journey. When we feign affection, we deny ourselves the opportunity to connect on a deeper level. We trade genuine relationships for shallow interactions and surface-level connections. True happiness and success cannot be achieved by deceiving ourselves and others; they can only be attained through authenticity and vulnerability.

To break free from the shackles of feigned affection, it is essential to cultivate self-awareness. Take the time to reflect on your own motivations, desires, and emotions. Understand that it is okay to have bad days, to feel vulnerable, and to show your true self. By accepting and embracing your own authenticity, you create an environment that encourages others to do the same.

desiderata Things Desire

It is vital to prioritize genuine connections. Strive to build relationships based on trust, empathy, and sincerity. Invest time in nurturing these connections, both online and offline. Engage in meaningful conversations, listen attentively, and show genuine interest in others' lives. By being authentic and open, you create a safe space for others to be themselves, fostering a sense of belonging and deeper connections.

Remember, perfection lies not in flawless appearances but in the imperfect beauty of real experiences. Embrace vulnerability, for it is through vulnerability that we cultivate strength. Let go of the need to impress others and instead focus on building relationships that nourish your soul. As you navigate the complexities of today's society, resist the temptation to feign affection, and strive for genuine connections that will enrich your life in ways far beyond the surface level.

Don't forget, living a perfect life requires authenticity and sincerity. Do not be afraid to show your true self, embrace your imperfections, and connect with others on a genuine level. Release the burden of feigned affection, and let your authenticity shine through. Only then will you discover the profound joy and fulfillment that comes from living a truly perfect life.

"Neither be cynical about love; for in the face of all aridity and disenchantment, it is as perennial as the grass."

desiderata Things Desire

Enduring Love

It is easy to become disillusioned and skeptical about the concept of love. We witness broken relationships, heartache, and the fleeting nature of many connections around us. It is no wonder that some may question the enduring power of love and its significance in our lives. However, it is precisely during these times of aridity and disenchantment that we must remember that love, like the grass, remains perennial.

When we say love is perennial as the grass, we draw upon the timeless wisdom of nature. The grass, no matter how harsh the winter or scorching the summer, possesses an unwavering ability to regenerate and grow. It endures, persistently spreading its vibrant greenness across the earth. Similarly, love has an innate capacity to persist and bloom even in the face of adversity.

In today's society, we often witness a cynicism that stems from past disappointments or a fear of vulnerability. We guard ourselves against hurt, building emotional walls that isolate us from the very connections that can enrich our lives. But in doing so, we deny ourselves the profound beauty and transformative power of love.

Love is not immune to challenges or setbacks. It requires effort, understanding, and forgiveness. Just as the grass needs sunlight, water, and nourishment to thrive, love needs care, communication, and commitment to flourish. Love is not a magical cure-all, but rather a force that requires cultivation and nurturing.

Today, more than ever, society needs a renewed appreciation for the perennial nature of love. In a world that often values instant gratification and disposability, we must remind ourselves of the depth and lasting impact that love can have. Love is not a fleeting emotion that comes and goes with the passing of time; it is a profound and enduring force that transcends the transient nature of our existence.

We see the power of love in the most remarkable acts of kindness and compassion. It is in the selfless dedication of individuals who devote their lives to helping others. It is in the unwavering support we receive from our loved ones during our darkest hours. Love has the potential to heal, inspire, and transform lives.

desiderata Things Desire

Embracing the perennial nature of love means recognizing that it is not always perfect or effortless. It means being willing to navigate the challenges, to put in the work required for its growth, and to accept the vulnerability that comes with opening ourselves to another. It means understanding that love is not solely about the destination but also the journey, and that the journey itself is what shapes and strengthens us.

In our society, where cynicism often prevails, let us choose to be believers in the power of love. Let us be the ones who sow seeds of kindness, understanding, and empathy. Let us water the garden of love with our actions, and watch as it thrives and spreads its roots deep into the soil of our existence.

Remember, just as the grass persists through the changing seasons, love endures through the highs and lows of life. It is perennial, steadfast, and capable of transforming not only our individual lives but also the world around us. By embracing the perennial nature of love, we can create a society that is defined by compassion, connection, and the belief in the extraordinary power of human connection.

"Take kindly the counsel of the years, gracefully surrendering the things of youth."

Embrace Aging Gracefully

The concept of living a perfect life often conjures images of eternal youth, boundless energy, and an unquenchable thirst for success. We are bombarded with messages that encourage us to cling desperately to our youth, to resist the natural process of aging, and to chase after an elusive fountain of eternal vitality. However, true wisdom lies in recognizing the value of each stage of life and gracefully embracing the changes that come with the passing years.

"Take kindly the counsel of the years" suggests that we should listen attentively to the wisdom that comes with age and experience. Our society often undervalues the elderly and dismisses their wealth of knowledge. However, it is through the accumulation of years that one gains insights, acquires a broader perspective, and develops a deeper understanding of life's complexities. By embracing the wisdom that the passage of time brings, we can avoid repeating the mistakes of the past and make more informed decisions for our future.

"Gracefully surrendering the things of youth" invites us to let go of the attachments and expectations that we often associate with our younger years. Youth is a time of exploration, experimentation, and boundless energy. It is a period marked by aspirations, dreams, and a relentless pursuit of personal goals. However, as we mature, it becomes essential to recognize that the priorities and values we held in our youth may evolve.

Society often places undue pressure on us to conform to certain standards, perpetuating the notion that youthfulness equates to happiness and success. We may find ourselves chasing after unattainable ideals, clinging to outdated dreams, or desperately clinging to the past. However, by gracefully surrendering the things of youth, we free ourselves from the burden of unrealistic expectations and allow room for personal growth, fulfillment, and contentment.

To live a perfect life in today's society, we must find a delicate balance between cherishing the enthusiasm and vitality of youth and embracing the wisdom and experience that age brings. It is not about resisting the natural process of aging but rather acknowledging that each stage of life offers unique opportunities for personal development and fulfillment.

So, how can we apply this wisdom to our lives today? Here are a few key considerations:

Embrace Lifelong Learning: Cultivate a mindset of continuous growth and curiosity. Seek out new experiences, expand your knowledge, and engage in activities that challenge you intellectually. Learn from those who have walked the path before you and be open to their counsel.

Value Relationships and Connections: As we age, the importance of meaningful relationships becomes increasingly evident. Nurture your relationships with family, friends, and mentors. Cherish the wisdom and guidance they offer and be willing to pass on your own knowledge to the younger generation.

Redefine Success on Your Terms: Society's definition of success may change as you grow older. Take the time to reflect on what truly matters to you and align your goals and aspirations accordingly. Embrace the freedom to redefine success based on your own values, passions, and priorities.

Embody Self-Care and Well-Being: As the years pass, taking care of your physical, mental, and emotional well-being becomes paramount. Prioritize self-care practices that promote longevity, vitality, and overall wellness.

Recognize the beauty and grace that come with embracing the natural changes in your body and mind.

Embrace a Purpose-Driven Life: Seek a sense of purpose and meaning that transcends the pursuit of youth-centric desires. Identify the values and causes that ignite your passion and make a positive impact on the world around you. Dedicate your time, skills, and resources to something greater than yourself.

By taking kindly the counsel of the years and gracefully surrendering the things of youth, we can navigate the journey of life with grace, wisdom, and a sense of purpose. Embrace the changes that come with each passing year, for within them lies the essence of a truly perfect life.

"Nurture strength of spirit to shield you in sudden misfortune."

Nurture Inner Strength

It is essential to nurture our strength of spirit to shield ourselves from sudden misfortune. Life has a way of throwing unexpected challenges our way, and it is our inner resilience and fortitude that determine how we navigate through these turbulent times. Developing and nurturing a strong spirit is not only crucial for our personal well-being, but it also enables us to face adversity head-on and emerge stronger than ever before.

So, what does it mean to nurture our strength of spirit? It means cultivating a mindset that embraces resilience, perseverance, and unwavering determination. It means harnessing the power within ourselves to rise above setbacks, setbacks that can often seem insurmountable. It means recognizing that setbacks and misfortune are not permanent states but temporary roadblocks on the path to success and personal growth.

desiderata Things Desire

In a society that often prioritizes external achievements and material possessions, nurturing strength of spirit reminds us to focus on our inner selves. It encourages us to build a strong foundation within, one that is not easily shaken by the storms of life. We live in a world where external circumstances can change rapidly, but our internal strength is what truly sustains us in the face of adversity.

Nurturing strength of spirit begins with self-awareness. Take the time to understand your values, passions, and purpose in life. When you have a clear understanding of what truly matters to you, you develop an unshakable core that guides your decisions and actions. This self-awareness acts as a shield, protecting you from the negative influences and distractions that can hinder your progress.

Another crucial aspect of nurturing strength of spirit is cultivating a positive and resilient mindset. Train yourself to see opportunities in every challenge, to view failures as steppingstones towards success, and to embrace growth and learning. Surround yourself with individuals who inspire and uplift you and seek out mentors who have faced their own misfortunes and emerged stronger. Their wisdom and guidance can be invaluable on your journey to personal and professional fulfillment.

In our society, where comparison and judgment often run rampant, nurturing strength of spirit also means embracing self-compassion and practicing empathy towards others. Understand that everyone faces their own unique struggles, and it is through compassion and understanding that we can foster connections and support one another during difficult times. By nurturing our own strength, we can become a source of inspiration and encouragement for those around us.

Lastly, remember that strength of spirit is not a fixed attribute but a continuous process of growth and development. Just as physical exercise strengthens our bodies, actively engaging in practices that nourish our spirits is vital. Whether it is through meditation, journaling, connecting with nature, or engaging in creative pursuits, find activities that replenish your inner well and provide you with the energy and resilience to face whatever comes your way.

In addition, nurturing strength of spirit to shield ourselves in sudden misfortune is of utmost importance. It means cultivating self-awareness, fostering a positive and resilient mindset, practicing self-compassion and empathy, and engaging in activities that replenish our inner strength. By nurturing our spirits, we not only fortify ourselves but also become beacons of hope and inspiration to others. Remember, you have the power within you to overcome any obstacle and create a life that is aligned with your highest aspirations. Nurture your strength of spirit and embrace the journey towards a fulfilling and purposeful life.

*"But do not distress yourself
with dark imaginings."*

Worry And Anxiety

Information bombards us from every direction and the pressure to succeed can be overwhelming, it is all too easy to fall prey to sudden imaginings that can lead us astray from living a perfect life. We are constantly bombarded with images of others' seemingly flawless lives on social media, and we find ourselves longing for their success, their happiness, their seemingly perfect existence. But here's the truth: perfection is an illusion, and chasing after it will only bring us distress.

When we distress ourselves with sudden imaginings, we create unrealistic expectations for ourselves. We envision a life without any challenges, where everything falls into place effortlessly. We imagine that success, happiness, and fulfillment are destinations we can reach without facing any obstacles along the way. But the reality is that life is a journey filled with ups and downs, triumphs and setbacks, and unexpected twists and turns. Embracing this reality is essential for our growth and well-being.

So, what does it mean to not distress yourself with sudden imaginings in today's society?

It means letting go of the unrealistic portrayals of perfection that inundate our screens. It means understanding that behind the meticulously curated social feeds and the carefully crafted success stories lies a deeper truth: nobody's life is perfect. Everyone faces struggles, failures, and imperfections. Those who have achieved great success have likely endured countless rejections, setbacks, and moments of self-doubt.

Instead of comparing ourselves to others' highlight reels, we should focus on our own journey and progress. Each one of us has a unique path to follow, filled with our own challenges and opportunities. It is in embracing our individuality, flaws, and imperfections that we find true fulfillment.

Moreover, not distressing ourselves with sudden imaginings means setting realistic goals and expectations. Rather than striving for an unattainable vision of perfection, we should set meaningful and achievable objectives that align with our values and passions. By focusing on our personal growth, rather than comparing ourselves to others, we can cultivate a sense of purpose and progress.

Remember, life's imperfections and challenges are what shape us and allow us to grow. They provide us with the opportunity to learn, adapt, and become stronger. When we distress ourselves with sudden imaginings of a perfect life, we are denying ourselves the chance to embrace the messy, beautiful, and authentic nature of existence.

Living a perfect life is not about achieving an unrealistic ideal or comparing ourselves to others. It is about embracing our unique journey, setting realistic goals, and finding fulfillment in the process. But do not distress yourself with sudden imaginings of a flawless existence. Instead, embrace the imperfections, setbacks, and unexpected detours that life presents. It is through these experiences that we discover our true potential and live a life that is truly meaningful.

desiderata Things Desire

"Many fears are born of fatigue and loneliness."

Fatigue And Lonliness

The pace of life seems to be accelerating at an unprecedented rate. We are constantly bombarded with information, responsibilities, and expectations. We find ourselves caught in a perpetual cycle of busyness, leaving little time for rest, reflection, and meaningful connections with others. It is within this context that we must explore the profound truth: many fears are born of fatigue and loneliness.

Fatigue drains our energy, both physically and mentally. When we are constantly running on empty, our ability to cope with challenges diminishes, and our fears loom larger than life. Exhaustion clouds our judgment, saps our motivation, and weakens our resilience. We become more susceptible to negative thoughts, self-doubt, and anxiety. It is in this depleted state that even the smallest obstacles can appear insurmountable.

In our increasingly interconnected yet isolated world, loneliness has become a pervasive issue. Despite being more digitally connected than ever before, genuine human connection has suffered. We find ourselves surrounded by virtual communities yet starved for genuine intimacy and meaningful relationships. Loneliness can infiltrate our lives, leaving us feeling disconnected, misunderstood, and unfulfilled. In this state of isolation, our fears multiply, taking on a life of their own.

Today, the effects of fatigue and loneliness on our fears are amplified. The constant demands of work, the pressure to succeed, and the never-ending stream of social media notifications all contribute to our fatigue. We are constantly connected but rarely truly present. This constant stimulation and lack of rest leave us perpetually drained, unable to find respite and recharge. It is within this depleted state that our fears can run rampant.

Simultaneously, the rise of social media has given us a skewed perception of reality. We compare our lives to carefully curated highlight reels of others, leading to feelings of inadequacy and isolation. Loneliness creeps in as we struggle to live up to the unrealistic expectations set by society and ourselves. We fear judgment, rejection, and failure, fueling a vicious cycle that perpetuates our fatigue and loneliness.

To overcome these challenges and conquer our fears, we must first acknowledge and address the role fatigue and loneliness play in our lives. We need to prioritize self-care and make time for rest and rejuvenation. This means setting boundaries, practicing mindfulness, and finding activities that bring us joy and replenish our energy. By nurturing ourselves, we can build resilience, regain clarity, and tackle our fears with renewed strength.

Furthermore, we must actively seek genuine connections with others. It is through meaningful relationships that we find support, understanding, and a sense of belonging. Connecting with like-minded individuals, joining communities centered around our passions, and engaging in heartfelt conversations are powerful ways to combat loneliness. Sharing our fears and vulnerabilities with trusted individuals can help us gain perspective and receive the support we need to face our fears head-on.

Right now, more than ever, the influence of fatigue and loneliness on our fears cannot be underestimated. Recognizing the impact of these factors is crucial to living a more fulfilling and fearless life. By taking the time to rest, replenish our energy, and cultivate genuine connections, we can break free from the cycle of fatigue and loneliness that fuels our fears. Embrace the power within you to transcend these challenges, and you will discover a life of purpose, resilience, and true happiness.

"*Beyond a wholesome discipline, be gentle with yourself.*"

Gentle Self-Compassion

We often find ourselves caught up in the pursuit of perfection. We strive for success, constantly pushing ourselves to achieve more, be better, and live a "perfect" life. We set high standards and hold ourselves accountable to strict discipline, believing that it is the key to attaining happiness and fulfillment. However, amidst this relentless pursuit, we often forget a fundamental truth: beyond a wholesome discipline, it is crucial to be gentle with ourselves.

What does it mean to be gentle with yourself in today's society? It means acknowledging your humanness, embracing your imperfections, and practicing self-compassion. It means understanding that you are a work in progress, and that self-improvement takes time, patience, and forgiveness.

In a world that bombards us with images of flawless beauty, constant achievements, and seemingly perfect lives, it's easy to fall into the trap of self-criticism and self-judgment. We compare ourselves to others, measuring our worth based on external benchmarks and societal expectations. This constant comparison creates a breeding ground for self-doubt and dissatisfaction. However, by being gentle with ourselves, we can break free from this destructive cycle.

Being gentle with yourself means treating yourself with kindness, understanding, and acceptance. It means acknowledging your strengths and celebrating your successes, no matter how small. It means recognizing that failure is a part of life and an opportunity for growth. It means giving yourself permission to make mistakes, learn from them, and move forward with renewed determination.

Moreover, being gentle with yourself involves nurturing your mental, emotional, and physical well-being. It means prioritizing self-care, setting healthy boundaries, and practicing mindfulness. It means taking time for activities that bring you joy and allow you to recharge. It means being aware of your limitations and knowing when to ask for help or seek support.

Beyond a wholesome discipline, being gentle with yourself also extends to cultivating a positive inner dialogue. Pay attention to the way you speak to yourself and challenge any negative or self-deprecating thoughts. Replace them with affirmations and words of encouragement. Treat yourself with the same kindness and compassion you would offer to a dear friend or loved one.

In our society, where perfection is often glorified, being gentle with yourself may seem counterintuitive. It is precisely in embracing our imperfections, our vulnerabilities, and our humanness that we find true strength and resilience. It is through self-compassion and self-love that we can create a life filled with authenticity, joy, and fulfillment.

Remember, beyond a wholesome discipline, be gentle with yourself. Embrace your uniqueness, celebrate your progress, and grant yourself the grace to navigate the ups and downs of life. By practicing self-compassion, you will cultivate a deep sense of inner peace and contentment, enabling you to live a truly fulfilling and purposeful life.

So, as you embark on your journey of success, remember to be kind to yourself. Embrace your flaws, learn from your mistakes, and cherish the remarkable individual that you are. Beyond a wholesome discipline, be gentle with yourself, and watch as your true potential unfolds.

"You are a child of the universe no less than the trees and the stars; you have a right to be here."

Of The Universe

It is easy to lose sight of our individual worth and the significance of our existence. We often find ourselves constantly comparing our lives to others, feeling inadequate and questioning our place in the world. In the midst of this chaos, it becomes crucial to remind ourselves of a profound truth: "You are a child of the universe, no less than the trees and stars; you have a right to be here."

These words hold a deep meaning that resonates with the human spirit. They remind us that we are not merely insignificant beings aimlessly navigating through life. Rather, we are an integral part of the universe, deserving of love, respect, and the opportunity to fulfill our unique purpose.

In our society today, it's easy to get caught up in the never-ending pursuit of external validation and societal expectations. We measure our worth based on superficial standards of success, appearance, and material possessions. But in doing so, we lose sight of our inherent value as individuals. We forget that we are interconnected with the universe, intimately woven into the fabric of existence.

Embracing the concept of being a child of the universe means acknowledging that you are not defined by external achievements or the opinions of others. It means recognizing that your existence is valuable in and of itself, regardless of your accomplishments or societal status. You have a right to be here, to occupy space and contribute your unique perspective to the world.

When you fully embrace this truth, you empower yourself to live authentically, guided by your own passions and aspirations. You free yourself from the shackles of comparison and societal pressures, allowing your true potential to unfold. It is from this place of self-acceptance and self-love that you can cultivate the life you desire.

Living as a child of the universe also means understanding the interconnectedness of all beings and the responsibility that comes with it. Just as the trees provide oxygen, the stars illuminate the night sky, and the rivers nourish the land, you too have a role to play in the grand tapestry of life. Your unique gifts, talents, and experiences contribute to the greater whole, creating a ripple effect that can inspire and uplift others.

Remember, in a society that often tries to diminish our sense of worth and convince us that we are not enough, it is crucial to embrace the truth of our existence. You are a child of the universe, no less than the trees and stars; you have a right to be here. Your presence matters, and your contributions are valuable.

So, as you navigate your journey through life, let these words serve as a guiding light. Embrace your uniqueness, honor your worth, and recognize the incredible power that lies within you. Step into the world with confidence, knowing that you have a right to be here, and your presence makes a difference.

Embrace the beauty of being a child of the universe, and watch as the world opens its arms to welcome you into a life of purpose, fulfillment, and endless possibilities.

"And whether or not it is clear to you, no doubt the universe is unfolding as it should."

Trust The Unfolding

We often find ourselves caught up in the whirlwind of constant change, overwhelming responsibilities, and the never-ending pursuit of perfection. We strive to achieve our goals, make a mark in the world, and live what we perceive as a perfect life. However, amidst the chaos and the pressure we put on ourselves, it is crucial to remember the profound wisdom embedded in the verse, "And whether or not it is clear to you, no doubt the universe is unfolding as it should."

In our fast-paced and interconnected world, it is easy to lose sight of the bigger picture. We become consumed by our desires for success, wealth, and recognition, forgetting that we are mere specks in the grand tapestry of the universe. We often overlook the fact that the universe operates at its own divine rhythm, constantly evolving and weaving together the intricate threads of our lives.

It is human nature to strive for control, to seek certainty and order in an inherently unpredictable world. We meticulously plan our lives, meticulously plot our path to success, and become disheartened when things don't go as expected. We forget that the universe has its own plans, its own timeline, and its own way of orchestrating events that ultimately shape our journey.

When we embrace the notion that the universe is unfolding as it should, we let go of the burdensome need to control every aspect of our lives. We surrender to the cosmic forces that guide us, trusting that every twist and turn, every triumph and setback, is a vital part of our personal growth and fulfillment. We understand that the universe has a way of nudging us in the right direction, even when it may not be immediately clear to us.

In today's society, where comparison and instant gratification permeate our lives through social media and constant connectivity, it is more important than ever to acknowledge that our individual journeys are unique and incomparable. We must resist the temptation to measure our lives against the highlight reels of others. Instead, we must find solace in the fact that our path is unfolding as it should, tailored precisely to our needs, aspirations, and soul's purpose.

It is through embracing the uncertainty and unpredictability of life that we find our true selves and unlock our greatest potential. Every setback is an opportunity for growth, every detour a chance to explore new territories, and every failure a steppingstone toward success. When we accept that the universe is unfolding as it should, we release ourselves from the shackles of self-doubt, anxiety, and fear of the unknown.

So, in this society where the pressure to achieve perfection is relentless, remember to pause, take a deep breath, and trust in the natural order of the universe. Remind yourself daily that you are a part of something greater, and the unfolding of your life is in perfect alignment with the cosmic dance of existence.

Embrace the uncertainties, cherish the detours, and have faith in the unseen forces that guide your journey. By surrendering control and aligning your intentions with the universe, you will discover a newfound sense of peace, purpose, and fulfillment.

And whether or not it is clear to you, no doubt the universe is unfolding as it should. Embrace this wisdom and let it guide you toward living a life that is not only successful but also deeply meaningful and authentically yours.

"*Therefore be at peace with God, whatever you conceive Him to be.*"

Harmonic Spirituality

Finding inner peace and a sense of purpose can seem like an elusive goal. We often face challenges, setbacks, and uncertainties that can shake our faith and leave us feeling disconnected from a higher power. However, regardless of our religious or spiritual beliefs, this verse's message lies in embracing a deeper understanding of ourselves and our place in the world.

A Higher Power, whatever you conceive Him to be, extends beyond the boundaries of religious doctrine or personal beliefs. It is a concept that transcends the confines of organized religion and invites us to explore the vastness of our inner selves. It encompasses a universal force, an energy that unites all living beings and interweaves our lives in mysterious ways.

In today's society, the notion of a Higher Power takes on a new meaning. We live in a world where diversity is celebrated, and people follow various religious, spiritual, or non-religious paths. This diversity provides an opportunity for us to embrace a more inclusive and open-minded perspective. We can acknowledge and respect the beliefs of others while discovering our own unique connection to something greater.

For those who believe in God, this message encourages you to find solace and comfort in your faith. Seek guidance from your religious teachings and scriptures, and let the divine wisdom inspire and uplift you. Embrace the rituals and practices that bring you closer to your understanding of a Higher Power.

However, for those who do not believe in a traditional religious God or follow a different worship belief, this message remains equally relevant. It invites you to explore spirituality in its broader sense—the exploration of the self, the interconnectedness of all life, and the quest for meaning and purpose. Your connection to a Higher Power can be found in nature, in acts of kindness, or in the pursuit of knowledge and personal growth. It can be a force that inspires you to be the best version of yourself and make a positive impact on the world.

To be at peace with a Higher Power, whatever you conceive Him, Her, or It to be, requires an open heart and a curious mind. It means embracing humility and acknowledging that there are aspects of life that are beyond our comprehension. It calls for the willingness to let go of rigid beliefs and be open to the infinite possibilities that exist.

Living a perfect life is not about attaining unattainable standards or conforming to societal expectations. It is about finding peace within ourselves and aligning our actions with our core values. It is about cultivating gratitude, kindness, and compassion towards ourselves and others. It is about being authentic, true to who we are, and living a life that is in harmony with our deepest convictions.

Being at peace with a Higher Power, whatever you conceive Him to be, means embracing the diversity of beliefs and finding unity amidst the differences. It means respecting others' paths while staying true to your own. It means acknowledging that we are all interconnected and that our actions ripple through the world, creating a collective impact.

So, as you navigate through the complexities of modern life, remember to seek peace within yourself. Embrace a Higher Power, whatever you conceive Him to be, and let it guide you on your journey. Embrace the wonders of existence and cherish the beauty of diversity. For it is in this state of peace, acceptance, and understanding that we can truly experience the richness and fulfillment of a life well-lived.

"*And whatever your labors and aspirations, in the noisy confusion of life, keep peace in your soul.*"

A Peaceful Soul

Finding peace within ourselves has become more challenging than ever before. We are constantly bombarded with external pressures and expectations that push us to achieve more, be more successful, and always stay ahead. Amidst this noisy confusion of life, it is crucial to keep peace with our souls and remain aligned with our true desires and values.

"And whatever your labors and aspirations, in the noisy confusion of life keep peace with your soul." These words hold immense wisdom, reminding us that while we strive for success, it is equally important to maintain a sense of inner tranquility and authenticity. True fulfillment comes from the harmony between our external achievements and the state of our inner being.

Society often defines success in narrow terms, focusing solely on external markers such as wealth, status, and recognition. However, the concept of a perfect life goes beyond these superficial measures. It encompasses a holistic approach that nurtures our physical, mental, emotional, and spiritual well-being.

Living a perfect life means pursuing our passions and goals while staying true to ourselves. It means aligning our actions with our core values, cultivating healthy relationships, and taking care of our physical health. It means finding balance in all aspects of our lives and making choices that bring us genuine joy and fulfillment.

In the pursuit of success, it is easy to lose sight of our inner voice. We may find ourselves chasing external validations or comparing our progress to others, leading to a sense of restlessness and dissatisfaction. However, if we allow the noise of the world to drown out our inner wisdom, we risk losing our authenticity and contentment.

To keep peace with our souls, we must make conscious efforts to create moments of stillness and reflection amidst the chaos. This may involve practicing mindfulness, meditation, or engaging in activities that nourish our spirits, such as spending time in nature, pursuing creative outlets, or connecting with loved ones.

Moreover, it is essential to define success on our own terms. Rather than adopting society's predefined notions, we must identify what truly matters to us. What are our passions, dreams, and aspirations? What brings us a deep sense of purpose and fulfillment? When we align our labors and aspirations with our soul's calling, we unlock a wellspring of motivation and enthusiasm that propels us towards our unique version of success.

Living a perfect life does not mean avoiding challenges or setbacks. Life will always present us with obstacles and uncertainties. However, when we keep peace with our souls, we develop an unwavering resilience and inner strength that help us navigate these difficulties with grace and determination.

In the midst of the noisy confusion of life, let us remember to tune into our souls and listen to the whispers of our hearts. By doing so, we embark on a journey towards living a perfect life, one that is harmonious, purpose-driven, and deeply satisfying.

So, let us strive for success, chase our dreams, and work tirelessly towards our goals, but never at the expense of our inner peace and well-being. Embrace the challenge of finding balance, and may your labors and aspirations always be guided by the serenity and wisdom of your soul.

"With all its sham, drudgery and broken dreams, it is still a beautiful world."

It's A Beautiful World

It's easy to get caught up in the chaos and lose sight of the beauty that surrounds us. We are constantly bombarded with images of success, glamour, and perfection, which can create unrealistic expectations and a sense of dissatisfaction with our own lives. However, amidst all the sham, drudgery, and broken dreams, it is crucial to remember that the world we live in is still undeniably beautiful.

What does it mean to live in a world filled with sham? Sham refers to the façade, the false pretenses that society often projects. We are often presented with carefully curated images on social media, portraying an idealized version of reality. It is easy to fall into the trap of comparison and believe that everyone else's lives are flawless, while ours are filled with shortcomings. However, we must recognize that these representations are just a small fraction of the truth. Behind the polished surface, there are struggles, imperfections, and challenges that everyone faces. By acknowledging this, we can free ourselves from the pressure of living up to an unrealistic standard and instead focus on our own unique journey.

Drudgery is another aspect of life that can make it seem less beautiful. The daily grind, the mundane tasks, and the repetition can sometimes drain our energy and enthusiasm. However, within the routine, there are opportunities for growth and transformation. It is through consistent effort and perseverance that we can achieve our goals and reach new heights. Instead of viewing drudgery as a burden, we can choose to see it as a steppingstone towards success. Every small task completed contributes to the bigger picture, and by finding purpose in even the simplest of actions, we can infuse our lives with meaning and fulfillment.

Broken dreams, too, can make the world appear less beautiful. We all have experienced setbacks, failures, and disappointments. It is during these moments that hope can waver, and the allure of a perfect life can fade away. But it is precisely in these times of struggle that our resilience is tested, and our character is forged. Our broken dreams serve as reminders of our ambition and determination. They propel us to redefine our goals, to learn from our mistakes, and to emerge stronger than ever before. When we embrace the lessons hidden within our broken dreams, we find the courage to continue chasing our passions, knowing that each failure brings us one step closer to success.

In our society today, the message that "with all its sham, drudgery, and broken dreams, it is still a beautiful world" resonates deeply. We are constantly bombarded by the superficial, the mundane, and the setbacks. However, beneath the surface, there is a tapestry of experiences, emotions, and connections waiting to be explored. It is in the simplest moments that we find the most profound beauty—a gentle breeze, a kind word, a shared laughter, or a helping hand. These moments remind us of the interconnectedness of all human beings and the incredible potential for joy and growth that lies within each of us.

Living a perfect life does not mean living a life without challenges, setbacks, or imperfections. It means embracing the full spectrum of human existence, with all its highs and lows, and finding beauty within it. It means acknowledging the sham, the drudgery, and the broken dreams while still cultivating an unwavering appreciation for the world around us.

As you navigate your journey towards success, remember that perfection is not the goal. Instead, seek to find fulfillment, purpose, and joy in the imperfect moments. Embrace the lessons that come with setbacks, view drudgery as an opportunity for growth, and recognize the beauty that exists even amidst the sham. For with all its sham, drudgery, and broken dreams, it is still a beautiful world, waiting to be discovered and cherished by those who dare to embrace its complexities.

"Be cheerful."

Cheerful Living

In a society characterized by constant busyness, high expectations, and relentless pressure, it's easy to get caught up in the pursuit of perfection. We strive to attain the perfect career, perfect relationships, and perfect lifestyles, often forgetting to cherish the simple joys of life. In this chapter, we will explore the significance of being cheerful, enjoying living, and resisting the urge to give in to worry. By embracing these principles, we can cultivate a sense of contentment and live a more fulfilling and perfect life in today's society.

Be Cheerful: Being cheerful is not about denying the challenges and difficulties we face but rather choosing to approach life with a positive attitude. It is about finding joy in the little moments, appreciating the beauty around us, and spreading happiness to others. Here's what being cheerful means in today's society:

Cultivate Positivity: Choose to focus on the positives in your life, even when faced with adversity. Look for the silver linings, find gratitude in the smallest of things, and maintain an optimistic outlook. This mindset not only enhances your own well-being but also influences those around you.

Spread Joy: One of the greatest gifts you can offer society is the ability to uplift others. Be a source of inspiration and motivation for those around you. Offer a listening ear, a genuine smile, and a kind word. Your cheerful demeanor can have a ripple effect, creating a positive and supportive environment.

Enjoy Living: Living a perfect life doesn't mean chasing an unattainable ideal; it means savoring the present moment, embracing imperfections, and finding fulfillment in the journey. Here's how you can enjoy living in toda"s society:

Have a Mindful Presence: Practice mindfulness and be fully present in each moment. Engage your senses and appreciate the simple pleasures life has to offer. Whether it's enjoying a delicious meal, taking a walk in nature, or spending quality time with loved ones, relish these experiences and let go of distractions.

Pursue Passions: Identify your passions and make time for activities that bring you joy. Whether it's painting, playing an instrument, or exploring the outdoors, engage in activities that ignite your soul. By following your passions, you infuse your life with purpose and find true fulfillment.

Don't Give in to Worry: Worrying is a common trap that hinders our ability to live a perfect life. It consumes our energy, clouds our judgment, and steals our joy. Here's how you can resist the urge to give in to worry:

Practice Acceptance: Accept that there will always be uncertainties and challenges in life. Instead of dwelling on what you cannot control, focus on what you can influence. Direct your energy towards finding solutions rather than worrying about the problem itself.

Develop Resilience: Cultivate resilience and learn to bounce back from setbacks. View failures as steppingstones to growth and see obstacles as opportunities for learning. By developing resilience, you can navigate the ups and downs of life with greater ease and maintain a positive outlook.

Being cheerful, enjoying living, and resisting worry are essential elements of living a perfect life. By adopting a positive mindset, embracing the present moment, and letting go of worry, you can create a life filled with contentment, purpose, and happiness. Remember, perfection is not found in an unattainable destination but in the ability to find joy in the journey. So, choose to be cheerful, relish the beauty of life, and let go of worry. Embrace the imperfections and celebrate the small victories along the way. This is the path to living a truly perfect life.

"Strive to be happy."

Find Happiness

In our quest for success and fulfillment, one word stands out amidst the noise and chaos of modern life: happiness. It is the ultimate destination, the purpose that underlies all our efforts and aspirations. In this chapter, we explore the profound significance of striving to be happy in today's society and uncover the essential ingredients for leading a truly fulfilling life.

Strive to be happy. These words hold great power, for they remind us that happiness is not a passive state to be stumbled upon, but an active pursuit that requires our conscious effort and dedication. In our society today, the pursuit of happiness can often be overshadowed by external pressures and societal expectations. We are bombarded with images of perfect lives, success defined by material possessions, and the constant comparison to others through the lens of social media.

However, true happiness cannot be found in the external world alone. It stems from within, from nurturing our mental and emotional well-being. It requires self-awareness, self-acceptance, and a commitment to personal growth. In our fast-paced society, it is easy to lose sight of these fundamental truths, but we must remind ourselves that genuine happiness lies in aligning our actions with our values and finding fulfillment in the present moment.

To strive to be happy in today's society means carving out time for self-care and reflection amidst the chaos of daily life. It means prioritizing our mental and physical health, cultivating meaningful relationships, and pursuing activities that bring us joy and fulfillment. It involves being mindful of the impact of technology and social media on our well-being and consciously creating boundaries to protect our mental and emotional space.

In this digital age, where the pursuit of success is often equated with accumulating wealth and material possessions, it is crucial to redefine our understanding of what it means to live a perfect life. True perfection lies not in the pursuit of external validation, but in embracing our imperfections, learning from our failures, and finding contentment in the journey towards personal growth.

Living a perfect life means aligning our goals and aspirations with our values and passions. It means pursuing work that brings us a sense of purpose and meaning, even if it doesn't conform to society's definition of success. It means nurturing our relationships, connecting with others on a deep and authentic level, and finding solace in the support and love of our loved ones.

Striving to be happy in today's society also involves embracing gratitude and practicing mindfulness. It means being present in each moment, savoring the simple pleasures, and finding beauty in the ordinary. It means shifting our focus from what we lack to what we already have, appreciating the abundance in our lives, and expressing gratitude for the small blessings that surround us every day. Here's what you can do to achieve happiness.

Cultivate a Positive Mindset: Happiness begins with your mindset. Choose to focus on the positive aspects of life and develop an optimistic outlook. Train your mind to see opportunities instead of obstacles, and practice gratitude for the blessings in your life. Embrace challenges as learning experiences, and let go of negative thoughts that hinder your happiness.

Pursue Meaningful Goals: Setting and pursuing meaningful goals gives you a sense of purpose and direction in life. Identify your passions and interests, and align your goals with them. When you engage in activities that bring you joy and fulfillment, you naturally increase your chances of experiencing happiness. Remember, it's not just about achieving the goals but also enjoying the journey.

Nurture Relationships: Human connection plays a vital role in our happiness. Surround yourself with positive and supportive individuals who uplift and inspire you. Invest time and effort in building and maintaining meaningful relationships with family, friends, and loved ones. Show kindness, empathy, and appreciation, as these qualities deepen connections and contribute to your overall happiness.

Practice Self-Care: Taking care of your physical, mental, and emotional well-being is essential for leading a happy life. Prioritize self-care activities that rejuvenate and replenish you. This can include regular exercise, nutritious eating, quality sleep, practicing mindfulness or meditation, engaging in hobbies, and finding time for relaxation. Remember, you cannot pour from an empty cup, so make self-care a non-negotiable part of your routine.

Embrace Resilience: Life is filled with ups and downs, and setbacks are inevitable. Embracing resilience allows you to bounce back from challenges and maintain your happiness in the face of adversity. Cultivate a growth mindset that sees failures as opportunities for growth and learning. Develop problem-solving skills, seek support when needed, and maintain a positive attitude even during tough times.

Live in the Present Moment: Happiness exists in the present moment, not in the past or future. Practice mindfulness by fully engaging in the here and now. Let go of regrets about the past and worries about the future. Focus on what you can control in the present and savor the simple joys of life. By living mindfully, you cultivate a deep appreciation for the present moment and increase your overall happiness.

Give Back and Practice Kindness: Helping others and practicing acts of kindness not only benefits those around you but also enhances your own happiness. Volunteer your time for causes you care about, lend a listening ear to someone in need, or simply perform random acts of kindness. By spreading positivity and making a difference in the lives of others, you contribute to a more compassionate world and experience a profound sense of fulfillment and happiness.

Ultimately, striving to be happy is a lifelong journey, and it requires our continuous effort and commitment. It is not a destination to be reached, but a way of life to be embraced. It is about finding balance, setting realistic expectations, and learning to let go of what is beyond our control. It is about making choices that align with our values and bring us closer to our authentic selves.

As we strive to be happy, let us remember that success and happiness are not mutually exclusive. We can achieve our goals and ambitions while maintaining our well-being and inner peace. By prioritizing our happiness and pursuing a life guided by our own definition of success, we can create a life that is truly perfect for us.

As you navigate the complexities of today's society, remember to strive to be happy. Embrace the journey, celebrate your victories, learn from your setbacks, and most importantly, prioritize your well-being. In doing so, you will discover that a life lived in pursuit of happiness is the most perfect life you can lead.

About The Author

Tim Northburg is an award-winning screenwriter and author of several fiction novels as well as multiple sales training and motivational guidebooks. He enjoys bringing his fantastical adventures to life through his adventure, fantasy, sci-fi books. His motivational books help people discover simple truths so they can live happy, fun, and successful lives. Tim Northburg enjoys writing non-fiction and fiction books of all kinds. He thrives on sharing his philosophy of success and motivation with others and he hopes his impact as a writer is thought provoking and fun. It is his long-term goal to inspire everyone to follow their dreams and achieve success in their lives.

www.TimNorthburg.com

For More Visit:

GALIFICATION MEDIA

Galification Media is committed to bringing high quality stories, in various genres and settings, to life through all forms of media from print to digital mediums as well as cinematic media.

Check out our other works at:

www.GalificationMedia.com

www.ingramcontent.com/pod-product-compliance
Lightning Source LLC
Chambersburg PA
CBHW060939040426
42445CB00011B/934